Left

MW01098748

SCHOOL PUBLISHERS

Photos:
Cover © MetaTools; p. 2, © Jeri Gleiter/Getty Images; p. 3, © MetaCreations/Kai Power Photos; p.4, © Corel; p. 5, © Photonica/Getty Images; p. 6, © PunchStock/DesignPics.com; p. 7, © Robert F. Sisson/Getty Images; p. 8, © MetaTools

Printed in China

ISBN 10: 0-15-358368-1
ISBN 13: 978-0-15-358368-1

Ordering Options
ISBN 10: 0-15-358355-X (Grade K Below-Level Collection)
ISBN 13: 978-0-15-358355-1 (Grade K Below-Level Collection)
ISBN 10: 0-15-360621-5 (package of 5)
ISBN 13: 978-0-15-360621-2 (package of 5)

4 5 6 7 8 9 10 0940 15 14 13 12 11 10 09

i

i

i

i

i

i

i